COMFORT *my* PEOPLE

Prayers and Reflections
Inspired by
the Venerable Matt Talbot

Tom Ryan

VERITAS

First published 2007 by
Veritas Publications
7/8 Lower Abbey Street
Dublin 1
Ireland

Email publications@veritas.ie
Website www.veritas.ie

ISBN 978 1 84730 030 0

Scripture quotations from the *New Revised Standard Version
Bible* © 1993 and 1998 by the Division of Christian
Education of the National Council of the Churches of
Christ in the United States of America.

A catalogue record for this book is available from the British
Library.

Printed in the Republic of Ireland by Betaprint Ltd, Dublin

Veritas books are printed on paper made from the wood pulp
of managed forests. For every tree felled, at least one tree is
planted, thereby renewing natural resources.

To my parents, Michael and Mary Ryan, who by their example shared the gift of faith with me.

To all who participate in our annual Matt Talbot Novena and for those who suffer from addictions.

Contents

Introduction:
The Matt Talbot Novena
in Clare

In the summer of 1992, I was appointed curate in the parish of Shannon. My then parish priest whom I succeeded ten years later, Canon Brendan O'Donoghue, asked me to become Spiritual Director of the Pioneer Centre in the parish. At the first meeting I attended, a discussion took place as to how the centre could best serve the needs of parishioners and, especially, respond in a spiritual manner to the growing problem of alcohol abuse. At the same time, in the Killaloe diocese, developments were taking place to promote adult religious education. I suggested to the centre that we would organise a nine-week Novena to the Venerable Matt Talbot, praying for all who were suffering from or sharing in the life of addictions. The thinking behind this was, as a spiritual organisation, the Pioneer

Association was offering a spiritual response in the community to the growing problem of coping with addiction. I also saw the Novena as serving the need for adult religious education, offering a time for prayer, reflection and coming together over a number of weeks.

In October 1993 our first session took place with six hundred people attending, and this continued for the next eight weeks with a different speaker each week leading people in prayer and reflection. The response of the people attending was very encouraging. Equally so was the great number of people who wrote asking to be remembered in prayer, telling their story of coping with addiction or living or working with someone with an addiction. These letters made us all more aware of the problem of the complexity and range of addictions that now exist.

The following year we repeated the experience and this time our colleagues in west Clare joined us, bringing together people from nine different parishes to a central venue in Kilrush Parish Church. We used the same preacher each week on different days and, between both centres, Kilrush and Shannon, 1,300 people were praying and reflecting together each week for nine weeks during the months of October and November.

This has continued each year since and, in recent years, the parish of Tulla has organised the Novena during Lent for the parishes of east Clare. Matt Talbot was chosen as a model because it was primarily through spiritual response that he got the strength to face and overcome the addiction in his life.

The story of Matt Talbot's struggle with his addiction is similar to the many stories of people today who are trapped by addictions of many kinds. This book of reflections is offered as a spiritual response to help people cope and to give hope. It is not a substitute to seeking and following professional intervention, be it medical treatment, counselling sessions or group support. It is offered in the context of wholeness where, if one part of the body is not right, then the whole body is affected. It is offered to complement the work that medical and professional centres offer to people seeking to be set free from their addiction.

The method this book uses is similar to that used in *Lectio Divina*, whereby we contemplate the words of a scripture passage and allow God's voice to speak to us. Thus, each reflection begins with a reading from scripture followed by some comments and observations. Each section then concludes with a prayer.

The book is divided into two parts: the first reflects on specific addictions such as the need to use alcohol or drugs, the compulsion to gamble or the uncontrolled need to work; the second part reflects on sources of spiritual support for those seeking help living with addiction or the addictive behaviour of another. It ends with a message of hope and blessing, believing that in the midst of the worst of times, God is with us to bless our movements and guide our steps. Matt Talbot is our inspiration as one who turned to God for help, and God did not let him down.

The Story
of Matt Talbot

Three things I cannot escape:
the eye of God, the voice of
conscience, the stroke of death.
In company, guard your tongue.
In your family, guard your
temper. When alone, guard
your thoughts.

Matt Talbot

For supporters of Gaelic games, 1884 is
remembered as the year that Michael
Cusack, from Carron in Co. Clare, founded
the Gaelic Athletic Association in Hayes
Hotel, Thurles, Co. Tipperary. It was also the
year that a young Dublin man, Matt Talbot,
at the age of twenty-eight, changed his life
completely.

On 19 September 1853, Charlie Talbot,
aged thirty, married Elizabeth Bagnall, in her

late teens, in Clontarf Church, Dublin. Both came from a working class background where poverty and excessive use of alcohol were prevalent. These were the years immediately after the Great Famine when people struggled just to survive.

Charlie and Elizabeth were parents to twelve children, nine of whom survived beyond infancy. Their second child, Matthew, was born on 2 May 1856. Matt's parents were good people who passed on a very solid faith to their children. The Talbot family were noted for their honesty and practice of the faith. While poor in the eyes of this world, they were rich in their love for God. Charlie was a good worker whose only weakness was that he drank too much, with inevitable consequences for his poor family. They lived at eighteen different addresses over a period of forty-one years. Through all their difficulties, the family prayed the Rosary together each day.

Matt, like so many other children of his time, did not avail of the opportunity for education offered by the new emerging religious orders and his school attendance was sporadic. He was eleven years old when he undertook a crash course in religious knowledge and what was then known as 'the Three Rs' but he was not a diligent student. In fact, the roll book of the Christian Brothers school in North Richmond Street where he attended for a year noted that he 'mitched' during much of his time there.

He had no interest in sport, literature, the arts or music. Lacking education, he frequently stole and was rough spoken. He was destined to join the countless number of unskilled labourers who drank heavily while attending to the externals of their religion by attending Mass on Sundays.

Matt began working at the age of twelve. His first job was with a wine merchant where he began sampling the drink he was bottling. One evening he came home drunk and his father changed his employment, hoping it would help. He moved to the Dublin Port and Docks Board, where he acted as a messenger, but his addiction to alcohol was further fuelled by the whiskey that was available to him in the bonded stores there. At seventeen he started work with Pemberton's as a builder's labourer.

By now Matt was a chronic alcoholic. His whole world completely centred on drink. Often this would involve telling lies, being self-centred, neglecting responsibilities and obligations. When Matt was drinking he became very hot-tempered, got into fights and swore.

Matt's drinking worried his mother deeply, as she could see her son following a pattern already set by his father. Matt began to suffer from hangovers, feelings of guilt and a sense of hopelessness. While he was still very conscientious about attending Mass on Sunday, he had already drifted from the Sacraments.

Workmen in those days were usually paid in the pub on a Saturday where most of their income was then spent, if it hadn't been already chalked up on credit or 'tick'. It was a regular feature of Matt's drinking that he would be broke on the Monday after payday. This meant that he was constantly on the slate for his alcohol supply. When his credit was all done, he would pawn his boots to buy drink, and was often spotted walking home from the pub in his bare feet.

From his early teens until the age of twenty-eight, Matt's only achievement was that he became a very heavy drinker. In 1884 he found himself out of work for a week and, with no money, he was unable to get any drink. His brothers, Phil and Joe, found themselves in the same position. Matt stood outside O'Meara's pub in the hope that his drinking friends, with whom he had often shared his money in the past, would return the favour. But they left him standing on the corner. Dejected and hurt, Matt made his way home.

He then made the biggest decision of his life. At the age of twenty-eight and at rock bottom, he told his mother that he was going to take the pledge. His mother prayed that he would have the strength to keep it. He went to Holy Cross College at Clonliffe and there he vowed to abstain from all alcoholic drink, initially for a three-month period. On that Saturday he also went to confession, followed by Mass and Holy Communion on Sunday. This was to become part of his daily life until his death.

It was by no means easy for him. He was still a builder's labourer in Pemberton's and was ridiculed by colleagues and so-called friends. While his mother prayed for strength for him, his former drinking pals expected him back in the pub at any time. Through the difficulties of withdrawal symptoms and the constant yearning for just one more drink, he turned to the presence of Jesus in the Eucharist and devotion to Our Lady through the Rosary for help to stay sober. He subjected himself to severe penance in the form of kneeling when praying, fasting for long periods and sleeping on timber planks with a board for a pillow. He attended Mass every morning before starting work at 6 a.m. During this time he tried hard to persuade his brothers to give up alcohol but to no avail. He took further pledges, leading eventually to his pledge to abstain from alcohol for the rest of his life. The Pioneer Total Abstinence Association of the Sacred Heart was founded in St Francis Xavier Church, Gardiner Street, Dublin, on 28 December 1898 by Fr James A. Cullen and Matt became a member in May 1890.

As time moved on, he was eventually conquering old temptations and bad habits. He learned to read and write, which opened many opportunities for him to read the psalms and the lives of the saints. He read biographies of St Teresa of Ávila, St Thérèse of Lisieux and St Catherine of Sienna. He also conquered discouragement and became obsessed with honesty. During his drinking years, he had stolen a fiddle from a poor musician, sold the fiddle and used the money to buy drink. In later life, he searched unsuccessfully for the man to try to make restitution for the theft. Matt was also a good singer and he loved to sing hymns in church at Mass and devotions.

Personal prayer took up a lot of his time each day and he was also being guided by a spiritual director. As he advanced more in his prayer and spiritual life, although he became more withdrawn, he was keenly aware of his fellow workers' struggle for social justice. He became a permanent employee of T&C Martin, where he worked in the timber yard as a labourer until his death. He joined a trade union, the Irish Transport and General Workers Union (ITGWU), now part of SIPTU. He gave all his wages to the needy and to the missions, keeping only the bare minimum for his meagre needs.

The true personality of Matt eventually began to shine in his truthfulness at all times, his loyalty to the faith, to his family and friends, and his sense of responsibility at work. His father died in 1899 at the age of seventy-three and Matt took good care of his mother until she died in 1915 at the age of eighty-one. Matt's mother died knowing that her prayers for her alcoholic son were answered. She had lived the last years of her life with him and experienced great joy, peace and happiness. Their story was very similar to that of St Augustine whose mother, St Monica, prayed for her son's conversion and he became living proof of the power of prayer. As St Paul reminds us, 'I can do all things in him who strengthens me' (Philippians 4:13).

Matt's decision to abstain for life from all alcoholic drink was the beginning of a long and challenging road. These changes in attitude were not miraculous; they took time, effort and a lot of soul searching. The practice of self-discipline was as hard for Matt as it is for all of us.

His prayer life was very much influenced by his membership and attendance at the Rosary Confraternity in the Dominican Church, the Sodality of Our Lady in the Jesuit Church in Gardiner Street and, for the last thirty-five years of his life, being a member of the Third Order of St Francis, known today as the Secular Franciscans, in Merchant's Quay. His daily attendances at Masses in various city-centre churches as well as his attendances at Missions and Retreats each year all helped him in his spiritual journey.

As a lay follower of St Francis of Assisi, Matt was very influenced by the way Francis made Christ the centre of everything; so too did Matt in his life. Matt formed by his participation in the Secular Franciscan way of life and Franciscan spirituality a life of love and sacrifice that appealed to him. A very simple approach to God by personal prayer and devotion to the Eucharist, Our Lady and the Stations of the Cross all helped to mould, encourage and guide Matt to achieve sanctity and a love of Christ and his mother.

In 1923, two years before his death, Matt was in hospital twice, with kidney and heart problems, and in the last few months of his life he suffered from chest pains and a shortness of breath. During these spells in hospital he continued his adoration of the Eucharist in the hospital chapel. In the eyes of the world, he was destitute; he drew from the National Health Allowance for twenty-six weeks the sum of fifteen shillings a week, after which he received a disability allowance. The local conference of St Vincent de Paul also supported him during this time, when he was out of work due to ill health.

In the spring of 1925, he returned to T&C Martin and continued to work there until the day before he died. On Trinity Sunday morning, 7 June 1925, he returned from early morning Mass to have a light breakfast which he had been doing since he had been in hospital and, as he returned to the 9 a.m. Mass in St Saviour's Church, Dominick Street, a twenty-minute walk for him, he collapsed on the path of Granby Lane; he died instantly. His death certificate stated heart failure as the cause of death.

His body was taken to the nearby Jervis Street hospital. He lay among strangers as there was no identification on him. It wasn't until the following day that his sister called to the morgue to formally identify him. Matt was sixty-nine years and one month when he died, a pauper, unknown and unidentified. On examination of his body at the time of death a cart chain was found around his waist with religious medals on it, a lighter chain around one arm and his Third Order of Saint Francis cord tied around the other arm. On one leg there was a light chain, with a rope tied around the other.

He was laid out in his Franciscan habit as a member of the Secular Franciscan and his remains were brought on the eve of Corpus Christi to the Jesuit Church of Saint Francis Xavier in Gardiner Street, where his funeral Mass took place on Thursday 11 June, the Feast of Corpus Christi. The burial took place in Glasnevin Cemetery.

In 1931, Archbishop Byrne of Dublin began the process of investigating his life. In 1952, his remains were exhumed from his grave in Glasnevin Cemetery and placed in a vault in the cemetery. Ten years later in 1962 his remains were brought to the Church of Our Lady of Lourdes in Sean McDermott Street where his coffin was placed in a granite tomb with the inscription 'The Servant of God, Matthew Talbot, 1856–1925'. Today, thousands of people visit this church and tomb each year, seeking Matt's intercession and praying for his canonisation.

Matt was not a colourful character; he had a very simple personality. He was a man who had great faith rooted in prayer and the Eucharist; he possessed a great sense of justice, especially for workers. Matt was a man who overcame addiction by using primarily the spiritual resources that are available to all who suffer addiction. He acknowledged that he broke his mother's heart on so many occasions, yet in his sobriety he did everything possible to make amends.

Matt was not a mentally ill man; the chains found on his body at death were very much a symbol of the great love he had for his faith. His conquering of addiction was with free will and the help of God. Today those who suffer from addictions or compulsions can and should avail of the necessary help of medical professionals. But the two ingredients of free will and of God's help are also still available to all in the journey of life and in the battle with addiction.

Matt's life and story is not time-bound. His story continues to be heard in our world today and it inspires the pages that follow.

LITANY FOR MATT TALBOT

A litany is an expression of solidarity with the whole people of God. Particularly, it is an expression of a shared ministry with those biblical or holy characters who have journeyed before us, a recognition that they have something to offer us and that we can be guided by their intercession. May this litany for Matt Talbot encourage and comfort all who pray it.

Lord have mercy, Christ have mercy.
Lord have mercy, Christ hear us.
Christ, graciously hear us.
God the Father of Heaven, have mercy.
God the Son, Redeemer of the world, have mercy.
God the Holy Spirit, have mercy.
Holy Trinity, One God, have mercy.

Holy Mary, pray for us.
Blessed Mother of God, pray for us.
Venerable Matt Talbot, born into poverty and lack, pray for us.
Venerable Matt Talbot, who suffered the abuse of an alcoholic father, pray for us.
Venerable Matt Talbot, who suffered

the loss of childhood innocence, pray
for us.

Venerable Matt Talbot, who
succumbed to the drug of alcohol as a
teenager, pray for us.

Venerable Matt Talbot, who fell into
debt due to his addiction, pray for us.

Venerable Matt Talbot, who stooped
to steal from a beggar, pray for us.

Venerable Matt Talbot, who later
searched in vain to repay the beggar,
pray for us.

Venerable Matt Talbot, whose faith
was darkened by the veil of addiction,
pray for us.

Venerable Matt Talbot, blessed by a
holy mother who never ceased
praying the rosary, pray for us.

Venerable Matt Talbot, who endured
intolerable cravings for alcohol, pray
for us.

Venerable Matt Talbot, whose friends
turned away from him in derision and
mockery, pray for us.

Venerable Matt Talbot, broken,
desperate, humbled, pray for us.

Venerable Matt Talbot, prostrate
before the tabernacle, tortured for
want of a drink, hearing only Jesus'

response, 'I thirst', pray for us.

Venerable Matt Talbot, restrained from receiving Eucharist by Satan, pray for us.

Venerable Matt Talbot, freed by Christ to receive Eucharist, pray for us.

Venerable Matt Talbot, upon crying out to Our Lady was freed from the bondage of an alcoholic obsession, pray for us.

Venerable Matt Talbot, who turned from sin to serve God's poor and destitute, pray for us.

Venerable Matt Talbot, who imposed upon himself severe penances to make reparation, pray for us.

Venerable Matt Talbot, who gave all to the poor, pray for us.

Venerable Matt Talbot, entirely transformed and sustained by the Holy Eucharist, pray for us.

Venerable Matt Talbot, so devoted to Our Lady that her rosary was ever in his hands, pray for us.

Venerable Matt Talbot, friend of Francis, Dominic and Ignatius, pray for us.

Venerable Matt Talbot, Third Order Franciscan, pray for us.

Venerable Matt Talbot, refuge and comfort for alcoholics and their families, pray for us.
Venerable Matt Talbot, totally embracing Christ's victorious grace in his life, pray for us.

Let us Pray

Venerable Matt Talbot, addict for Christ, look down upon all of us in our struggles with different addictions, in bondage, tortured of soul, heart and mind, blind to the saving light of Christ. Through your prayers, let us have our eyes opened by grace to see salvation in the Holy One of God, who hung upon a Cross so that we may be set free. Father, pour out your light and blessing in the name of your Son, Jesus Christ our Saviour. Amen.

PART I

REFLECTIONS ON ADDICTIONS AND COMPULSIONS

1

Bent Double and Unable to Stand Upright: Addiction to Alcohol and other Substances

One Sabbath day Jesus was teaching in the synagogue, and there was a woman present who, for eighteen years, had been possessed by a spirit that left her enfeebled: she was bent double and quite unable to stand upright. When Jesus saw her he called her over and said, 'Woman, you are rid of your infirmity' and he laid his hands on her. And at once she straightened up, and she glorified God. But the synagogue official was indignant because Jesus had healed on the Sabbath, and he addressed the people present. 'There are six days,' he said, 'when work is to be done. Come and be healed on one of those days and not on the Sabbath.' But the Lord answered him. 'Hypocrites!' he said. 'Is there one of you who does not untie his ox or his donkey from the manger on the Sabbath and take it out for watering. And this woman, a daughter of Abraham whom Satan has held bound these eighteen years – was it not right to untie her bonds on the Sabbath day?' When he said this, all his adversaries were covered with confusion, and all the people were overjoyed at the wonders he worked.

Luke 13:10-17

Each year, many people write with petitions and prayers of thanksgiving to the Venerable Matt Talbot Novena. The common thread throughout is that addiction to alcohol and other substances causes much pain and suffering in people's lives.

BENT DOUBLE AND UNABLE TO STAND UPRIGHT

Addiction can be defined as the 'uncontrolled, compulsive use' of a substance. People who are addicted are so utterly in the grip of that substance or behaviour that they are unable to stop seeking it, despite the harm it causes to their health, family life, job and friendships. Another description of addiction is that it is the state of being 'devoted to something'. This strikes me as an unusual but insightful description of addiction: unusual in that to be devoted implies something that is positive and benign. It does not immediately evoke an awareness of danger or threat. And yet it is an insightful description because to become devoted to something first suggests that one must feel that it provides a net gain, adding something very good to one's life. This is something that can often be forgotten in the midst of warnings about the dangers of alcohol, drugs, cigarettes and so on – that initial experiences of such things can be exhilarating, a 'falling in love' experience that, it seems, would make total sense to repeat. Thus, devotion is probably a good way to describe the addict's relationship with the addictive substance. The person becomes devoted to recapturing that first high, the thrill of those initial experiences when they fall in love with the feeling created by the alcohol or other drug. Yet so often, devotion turns to desolation and becomes an elusive quest which ends in a lonely place far removed from the original buzz.

Alcohol is indiscriminate in its victims and its misuse can wreak havoc amongst all ages, ethnic groups and social classes. Media images of young people falling down drunk on the streets in the early hours of weekend mornings are now commonplace. Hospitals and treatment centres report that the age profile of those afflicted by alcohol dependency is falling dramatically with increasing numbers of young women in particular risking liver disease, infertility and the other health problems associated with alcohol misuse.

But while the current spotlight falls on the behaviour of the young, we know that behind the doors of many homes, countless lives of all ages continue to be blighted by the persistent over-consumption of alcohol so that it is now recognised as a national epidemic.

If the abuse of alcohol can be viewed as perhaps the greatest threat to national health, the increased availability, affordability and acceptability of illicit drugs make them a ready contender for this dubious crown. Despite regular seizures by gardaí, we hear of the country being 'awash with drugs' and know that the purveyors of this lucrative trade continue to prey on the poor and seduce the vulnerable so that lives are destroyed and communities torn asunder.

And then there are the drugs which are completely legal and available in shops and pharmacies countrywide. These are the over-the-counter and prescription drugs whose purpose is to aid health and well-being but whose abuse can result in the breakdown of psychological and physical health.

Finally there is that most ubiquitous of drugs: cigarettes. Although not comparable to the others in terms of its ability to destroy the fabric of a life and the relationships therein, the health impact of addiction to nicotine is one with which we are all familiar; its link to heart disease, stroke and a variety of cancers is regularly highlighted. And while Ireland is to be commended for taking the lead in being the first European country to ban smoking in public places, much still needs to be done to eradicate the allure of this most damaging of drugs.

However one's life has been affected by substance addiction, whether directly or indirectly, there is no disputing the pain and suffering that comes after the initial high becomes elusive and when the substance is needed just to feel normal.

Like the woman in our gospel passage who was bent double, incapable of standing upright, many display the scars of their addiction on their bodies and in their faces.

Behind the signs that are visible to the eye are the spiritual and emotional costs: the loss of control and the feelings of fear and guilt. It is little wonder that many live in denial of the true nature of their addiction and that substances become attractive and compelling anaesthetics that dull the hard realities of life.

Matt Talbot shared similar emotions in his life; the indignity of pawning his boots to buy alcohol must have caused deep feelings of shame and guilt. He is an example of an addict who was jolted into a clear realisation of his situation. He saw the shallowness of his drink-related friendships and the toll that his way of life was having on his mother. That moment of clarity was the catalyst for change in his life. The road to recovery involved confronting the people and places associated with his drinking and overcoming the temptations to relapse. His life became a testament to willpower, self-honesty and absolute trust in God's help.

BENT DOUBLE AND UNABLE TO STAND UPRIGHT

PRAYER

Lord, as I reflect on the life of the Venerable Matt Talbot, you speak to me through him. Mindful of the part addiction has played in my own life I now come into your presence. Free me of all that weighs me down and bends me over. Help me to face the future with confidence, knowing that you call to me, uttering the same words you said to the woman in the Gospel: 'you are rid of your infirmities.' Teach me that the love you had for your servant Matt Talbot is the same love that I enjoy on my journey of life. My journey has sometimes led me to a valley of tears, but guided by your love I know I can reach the mountaintop where I too will experience the joy of all the wonders you can work. Give me courage, take my hand and strengthen my belief that with your help, nothing is impossible.

Venerable Matt Talbot, pray for us.

2

Come To Me, You Who Are Overburdened: Gambling

Come to me, all you who labour
and are overburdened and I will
give you rest. Take my yoke
upon you and learn from me, for
I am gentle and humble in
heart, and you will find rest for
your souls. Yes, my yoke is easy
and my burden light.

Matthew 11:28-30

There has always been need to treat
gambling with extreme caution. Today, there
are more reasons than ever to give serious
consideration to the trap that gambling can
become and to its disastrous consequences
for family life and for the life of the
individual. The opportunities to gamble
away large amounts of money are increasing

rapidly as technology allows us to gamble, without restraint, from the comfort of our own home using our phone, home computer or mobile. Television too offers countless opportunities to gamble at all hours of the day and night as television companies come up with more ways to encourage their audiences to phone in to quiz shows, thus creating a sizeable profit for the programme makers with comparatively little reward for the viewers.

So what is at the root of the urge to gamble? Though gambling in its extreme form is not a physical addiction like drug taking or alcohol addiction it shares some common characteristics with these addictions. Like alcohol or drugs, gambling promises to provide a distraction from the difficult lives that we lead. People who gamble speak of the buzz of laying a bet and the thrill of waiting to see if they will be lucky. Gambling, therefore, appeals to that part of us which seeks escapism and some gamblers become addicted, not primarily to the prospect of instant money, but to the excitement of taking a risk.

Nevertheless, there is no disputing the appeal of tangible financial reward and the possibility of being able to afford luxuries that we can only dream of without having to take the long route of hard work and effort. Anyone who has placed a bet on the Grand National can relate to the feeling of excitement that comes when success seems within reach. More of us know the feelings of despondency when we realise that our chance of success is gone. It is easy to imagine the highs and lows that are constant themes in the life of the gambling addict.

A particular danger of gambling singles it out from other addictions. The drinker can only consume a finite amount at any one time with the result being that the decline of the alcoholic is usually relatively slow. The gambler, on the other hand, can gamble an infinite amount of money in a very short time. Stories of people losing everything in a weekend of gambling are not just the stuff of myth. The hope of instant wealth so often turns to abrupt financial ruin.

Gambling, like most other addictions, is not just an individual affliction. Gambling addicts are products of our society rather than being different from the mainstream. The gambling industry is a multi-billion euro concern and is growing rapidly. That growth is fuelled by the proliferation of quiz shows, lotteries and other betting opportunities.

COME TO ME,
YOU WHO ARE OVERBURDENED

National governments earn many millions from taxes on betting and from the national lottery. This inevitably curbs their enthusiasm for tackling the growth in gambling. Thus, the misery it can visit on its victims, who often gamble because they are in desperate financial straits in the first place, continues unabated.

As gambling is both an international business and a transnational problem, the solutions to limiting its excesses need to have an equally transnational dimension with governments exerting more control over betting that takes place via the internet and satellite television. Yet, whichever measures governments put in place, these will only be effective for the individual if he or she is helped to understand the source of their behaviour through accessing the proper medical and peer support such as that offered by family doctors, addiction therapists and organisations like Gamblers Anonymous. And as the life of Matt Talbot exemplifies, and our scripture passage suggests, all who suffer the pain of addiction or compulsions can also rely on support for their tired spirits through the love and compassion of God who invites us all to bring our burdens to him, to trust in his mercy, and he will give us rest.

PRAYER

Heavenly Father, you invite and encourage us to come to you with our troubles. We come to you now, praying for all who are burdened with gambling addictions. Release them from the trap of compulsion, guide them and give them courage.

Help us all to realise that the riches which this world offers are passing and that the great prize of the eternal is worth striving for on the journey of life.

May Matt Talbot, who experienced temptation in his struggle with addiction, help all afflicted in this way to overcome their own trials and temptations.

Venerable Matt Talbot, pray for us.

3

Created in God's Image:
The Misuse of Food

> God created man in the image
> of himself, in the image of God
> he created him, male and
> female he created them. God
> blessed them, saying to them,
> 'Be fruitful, multiply, fill the
> earth and conquer it'. God saw
> all that he had made and indeed
> it was very good.

Genesis 1:26-27, 31

Being able to savour and appreciate food in
all its variety and flavour is a wonderful gift.
There is nothing better than enjoying a good
meal at home or in a favourite restaurant.
Indeed, table companionship is at the centre
of family life and of our Christian faith as we
gather to celebrate the Eucharist.

It is difficult, however, to fail to notice that for many in our society their relationship with food has become imbalanced and out of sync either through over-eating or under-eating. Expert reports frequently warn of the rise in obesity, while at the other end of the spectrum we are made aware of people who have become so afraid of weight gain that they limit their food intake to dangerously low levels.

There are complex reasons why some people's relationship with food leads to illness and addiction. But many who suffer in this way tell us that what lies at the heart of their eating disorders are painful life experiences that cause low self-esteem and a perception that they are just not good enough. Perhaps someone has suffered the terrible trauma of a tragic loss, the distressing rejection brought about by the breakdown of a relationship or the experience of being constantly criticised by an over-exacting parent, partner or employer. It is not difficult to see how these or other adverse life experiences could contribute to a poor self-image and low self-confidence. Whatever the catalyst, the result for some is that they turn to food and use it in a way which brings momentary control through bingeing or purging, but which ultimately causes self-harm and self-torment.

While there are a variety of individual reasons why a person's relationship with food becomes distorted, it is also important to recognise the contribution that wider society makes to a dysfunctional attitude to food. Consider for a moment the number of television advertisements that promote fast food which is cheap but usually lacking in nutritional value and unhealthy if eaten too often. Think of the super-size portions and the 'all you can eat' offers that some food outlets promote. Who is most likely to be attracted by such incentives? Inevitably it will be those with little disposable income who cannot afford the comparative expense of healthier food. And it will also be children and the young who are still unable to make informed choices about what is in their best interest. Thankfully, however, some governments are now beginning to recognise the health dangers of unregulated advertising by food and confectionary manufacturers and are planning to restrict the promotion of junk foods and drinks during children's programming.

Another feature of today's society is that we live in a time that seems to be obsessed with image. Young woman are told that size zero is what they need to aspire to. Air-brushed celebrities and emaciated models are portrayed as the norm. Television programmes badger people to look ever younger and profile painful cosmetic procedures and invasive surgeries as though they were run-of-the-mill trips to the dentist.

We also live in a world where many people are now considered to be 'time poor'. The pace of life is such that countless people complain of being over-stressed through trying to fit too many things into one day. Often, the first casualty is a healthy diet as people resort to eating time-saving but calorific snacks and ready-meals.

In all the examples above, a scenario is portrayed where people, whether through painful life experience, subtle marketing or societal and peer pressure, are persuaded to act against their own best interests in the way they treat food. In essence, they fail to recognise and accept the message stated so clearly in our scripture passage – that each of us is created in God's image and that indeed we are 'very good'. If we really accepted the truth of our own innate goodness, of the way that God views us as precious in his eyes, it would surely go a long way to fortifying us against the things in life that tell us that we don't measure up, that we don't make the grade.

When asked what is the greatest commandment, Jesus replied, 'You must love the Lord your God with all your heart, with all your soul and with all your mind. This is the greatest and first commandment. The second resembles it: You must love your neighbour as yourself' (Matthew 22:37-39). Jesus presupposed that we do indeed love ourselves. Of course, his was not an endorsement of selfishness or egotism. It was, rather, a recognition that in order to love others, one must also love oneself. To love oneself means to recognise one's absolute value. It also means accepting one's weaknesses and beginning to overcome them, not through self-punishment, but through accepting oneself as a unique and precious child of God, deserving of compassion, reverence, dignity and respect.

Matt Talbot's life offers hope to all who despair of overcoming self-destructive behaviours. His trust in God as a God of love and forgiveness led him to re-order his priorities and renew his life. It is a path that is open to all of us as we move forward on our own journeys. One step on this road is to

take courage and to begin to see ourselves
through the eyes of the God who loves us
exactly as we are.

PRAYER

Heavenly Father, you give us food
and drink so that we might live more
freely and creatively, yet we nourish
ourselves with much that is not life-
giving. Your son, Jesus, came to set us
free, to unblock all that is weighing
us down. Hear the prayer we make for
all who find the gift of food a
challenge, those who overeat and
those who have no desire to eat for
fear of the consequences.

You have taught us to be concerned
about people who are hungry and
who hunger for what is right: help us
now to be generous with our time,
our resources and our love. We know,
Lord, that in following the example
of Jesus, all our needs will be
supplied.
May the example of Matt Talbot,
who placed his trust in you at his

darkest hour, help all who are
struggling to see the food you offer us
as your gift to sustain us both in body
and soul.

Venerable Matt Talbot, pray for us.

4

Slow Me Down, Lord:
The Need to Stop and Rest

Jesus came to a village, and a woman named Martha welcomed him into her house. She had a sister called Mary, who sat down at the Lord's feet and listened to him speaking. Now Martha, who was distracted with all the serving, said, 'Lord, do you not care that my sister is leaving me to do the serving all by myself? Please tell her to help me'. But the Lord answered: 'Martha, Martha,' he said, 'you worry and fret about so many things, and yet few are needed, indeed only one. It is Mary who has chosen the better part: it is not to be taken from her.'

Luke 10:38-42

One of the most accepted addictions for people today is the addiction to work and to activity. The over-commitment of the 'workaholic' is often greeted with approval and such imbalance is seen as a virtue. An extreme work ethic is interpreted as a sign of great dedication and selflessness so that when we hear of people working eighteen hours each day we see it almost as something to be admired.

This addiction is not just confined to high-flyers and leaders of industry and commerce but is something that can affect all sectors of the workplace. It can also be evident in the home. It is all about feeling unable to stop and to do nothing. Reasons for this over-activity may be varied: the pressure that people feel to compete; the need for some level of job security in a company which prizes 'being married to the job'; an inability to say 'no' for fear of being seen as lazy or unwilling; an identity which is built around feeling indispensable or achieving in employment; a self-worth so caught up in having the perfect, spotless house that one is unable to leave the mess for another day.

St Luke's gospel story of activity and fuss is one that many of us can identify with from our own experience of life at home. Just picture the scene: Mary is sitting there calmly, hanging on to every word that Jesus spoke. Martha, on the other hand, is running around, trying to get the meal ready. Despite Martha's protest, we are told that Mary had chosen the 'better part'. We might be forgiven for thinking that Mary took the 'easy' part!

But Jesus was not denigrating work nor was he saying that the work which needs to be attended to should not be shared. Rather, he was calling on Martha, and on us, to stop and look at life and to try to keep it in balance. There is a time to work, but there is also a time to rest.

We can all be guilty of being too busy at times. But if we don't stop, it will become impossible to have real clarity of thought or to notice what is crying out for recognition in our lives. We risk neglecting the people we love, ignoring the things we may need to change and failing to make time to deal with the challenges that face us.

The third commandment instructs us to keep holy the Sabbath day, reminding us of the sacredness of rest and reflection:

Remember the Sabbath day and keep it holy. For six days you shall labour and do all your work, but the seventh day is a Sabbath for the Lord your God. You shall do no work that day, neither you nor your animals nor the stranger who lives with you. For six days the Lord made the heavens and the earth and the sea and all that these hold, but on the seventh day he rested; that is why the Lord has blessed the Sabbath day and made it sacred. (Exodus 20:8)

For some, the instruction to 'keep holy the Sabbath' may evoke memories of 'getting Mass in' on a Sunday morning. Sadly, for some people too, it may hold painful memories of a rule-bound system that they can no longer feel comfortable with in their lives.

But there are other ways of looking at these insightful words of scripture. They can be seen as an invitation to embrace the human need to rest and take stock of the important relationships in our lives – our relationship with ourselves, with our family and friends, with our community and with God.

In common parlance the word 'recreation' means to do things we enjoy –

to go for a stroll, read a book, go to the gym. Viewed at a deeper level, the word can be seen as two distinct words which mean to create again, to restore or make new. Some people might use their recreation time to devote a little bit more time to prayer, allowing God to pour his spirit into their hearts when they are silent and reflective. We all need this space in our lives to be re-created, refreshed and renewed. Like Mary in the gospel passage, we need to choose the better part and not have it taken from us.

In his earlier life Matt Talbot could find very little meaning in anything but drink. His early days of employment centred on working to get money for drink and drinking to forget about work. One was feeding the other in a vicious circle. How true is this for so many today. Work and busyness can turn into addictions which fuel other compulsive behaviours – consider the man driven by his need to succeed who works all hours and then uses drink to unwind until it too becomes a problem. Popular magazines are filled with stories of celebrities who develop dependencies on drugs and alcohol through trying to cope with the excesses of their working lives.

When we do not accept God's gracious invitation to rest, we can very easily end up relying on all kinds of dangerous activity to help us cope with life and living. The Lord himself told us that we were not made for the Sabbath, but that the Sabbath was made for us. God, in his wisdom, knows our need for a Sabbath in our lives; he knows we need rest to be re-created.

PRAYER

Lord, our God, our time is in your hands, our time for work and our time for rest. Help us to use the time given to each of us to good effect. Slow us down, help us to stop and observe, to think and to pray. Help us to appreciate all the blessings that surround us in the beauty of people, nature and all that you created. Slow us down, Lord; help us to hear the pondering of our heart through the easing of our mind. Slow us down, Lord, slow us down.

Venerable Matt Talbot, pray for us.

5

Treasure in Heaven: The Relentless Pursuit of Pleasure

He was setting out on a journey when a man ran up to him, knelt before him and put this question to him, 'Good master, what must I do to inherit eternal life?' Jesus said to him, 'Why do you call me good? No-one is good but God alone. You know the commandments: You must not kill; You must not commit adultery; You must not steal; You must not bring false witness; You must not defraud; Honour your father and mother'. And he said to him, 'Master, I have kept all these from my earliest days'. Jesus looked steadily at him and loved him, and he said, 'There is one thing you lack. Go and sell everything you own and give the money to the poor, and you will have treasure in heaven; then come, follow me'. But his face fell at these words and he went away sad, for he was a man of great wealth.

Mark 10:17-22

Traditionally, addiction has been viewed as possible only when one has a dependence on alcohol or some other drug. Over time, it has become accepted that one does not have to have a physical dependency for one to become addicted, such as in the cases of gambling and work that we have already considered.

But there is a range of other behaviours that ultimately cause significant harm to individuals and to the quality of their relationships which could fall into the broad category of addiction to pleasure. Examples include compulsive sexual activity which degrades and exploits, putting health at risk. There is the addiction to sport and exercise, which proves counter-productive to keeping fit by placing excessive strain on the body. There is the addiction to consumerism and over-spending, often resulting in amassing huge debts and precipitating crises in family life along similar lines to that of gambling. As with gambling and the misuse of food, we can look to commercial interests to take some of the responsibility for the growth of massive consumer debt as advertisers persuade us to live in a throwaway age and to spend more and more on the latest must-have gadget. And all the while instant credit allows the pain of paying to be postponed. The explosion in ways to communicate has also produced addictive behaviours as people spend countless anonymous hours talking to strangers in internet chat rooms, perhaps continually failing to notice the family member or neighbour who also needs their time and attention.

This far from exhaustive list denotes behaviours which, if they become persistent, lead, like other addictions, to an avoidance of reality and provide unhealthy distractions from the responsibilities and ordinariness of everyday life. By pursuing individual pleasures at any cost, people attempt to avoid pain and put meaningful relationships at risk by becoming divorced from reality and emotionally inaccessible to those closest to them.

Our gospel passage reminds us that sometimes life demands hard choices of us. We may not be asked to sell all we have and give it away but we will certainly be asked to face up to the realities and commitments of our lives and not create lives of fantasy in which we convince ourselves that what we engage in is harmless. Like those who relentlessly pursue what gives them pleasure, the rich young man had one major weakness which prevented him from becoming the person he wanted to be. Jesus did not condemn him for his weakness. Instead, showing unswerving tenderness and compassion, we are told that he loved him. And this fortifying love is ours also as Jesus looks at the weaknesses of our lives with complete understanding and empowering acceptance.

Later in the gospels, we see Jesus himself face the ultimate choice in the Garden of Gethsemane. In desolation, we hear him pray 'if it is possible, let this cup pass me by' (Matthew 26:39). His is a prayer that many can relate to when the harshness and pain of life pushes us down blind alleys that seem to offer sanctuary and relief. But when apparent sanctuary comes through extremes of behaviour such as those mentioned, then the relief is transitory and the human cost exorbitant.

Let us take heart from Matt Talbot who, to those who did not know of his suffering, appeared to be motivated solely by the pursuit of his own pleasure. Let us walk in his footsteps and learn from the courage which carried him beyond the slavery of his condition into a life of selflessness in the service of others.

PRAYER

O God, our loving father, in the past loving oneself was not stressed much. Teach us to love ourselves and to be comfortable with ourselves for unless we can do this, we cannot fulfil the great command to love you and love others.

You have made us in your own image and likeness and you love us unconditionally, with all our faults and failings. As Matt Talbot, you remind us that, despite our

difficulties, you continue with us on
life's journey, even at the times when
we fail to recognise you in our lives.
Renew our faith and trust in your
loving guidance and care for each
one of us as we try to live by the light
of your love.

Venerable Matt Talbot, pray for us.

PART II

SOURCES OF SPIRITUAL HELP FOR ALL

6

Be Reconciled:
Forgiveness

The Scribes and Pharisees
brought a woman along who
had been caught committing
adultery; and making her stand
there in full view of everybody,
they said to Jesus, 'Master, this
woman was caught in the very
act of committing adultery, and
Moses has ordered us in the Law
to condemn women like this to
death by stoning. What have
you to say?' They asked him this
as a test, looking for something
to use against him. But Jesus
bent down and started writing
on the ground with his finger.
As they persisted with their
question, he looked up and said,
'If there is one of you who has

not sinned let him be the first one to throw a stone at her'. Then he bent down and wrote on the ground again. When they heard this they went away one by one, beginning with the eldest, until Jesus was left alone with the woman, who remained standing there. He looked up and said, 'Woman, where are they? Has no one condemned you?' 'No one, sir,' she replied. 'Neither do I condemn you,' said Jesus, 'go away, and don't sin any more.'

John 8:1-11

When we apply for a mortgage, a job, or something else that will be very important in our lives, we all feel a bit apprehensive. If we could know in advance that the person who decides the outcome would be a kind person, full of understanding for our situation then it would surely lighten our burden.

Whatever the uncertainty of the situation in which we find ourselves in society, our situation before God is very different. When we approach God, we can be sure of a compassionate response. In the gospel passage, Jesus challenges those who wish to condemn the women by asking them to consider first their own flawed humanity. It is a lesson for all, teaching us to be slow to pass judgement on the actions of another.

Our God is the Father of Jesus who said there is more joy in heaven over one sinner who repents than ninety-nine who need not repent. Matt Talbot is a prime example. When he realised the love God had for him, he was able to stop his drinking and turn his life around. In doing so, he experienced a joy in his life that enabled him to live selflessly and generously.

Many good people who practice their religion and live exemplary lives often fail to experience such joy, finding it difficult to really experience the love of God in their lives. I often wonder how this can be and I find the answer in the chalice. A chalice is simply a cup, an old fashioned one, but to fill the cup you must first make sure that it is empty. Our hearts and lives are like chalices. To fill our hearts with love, we first have to make sure that they are empty of bitterness, anger, hatred and resentment. The more these issues are part of our lives, the less room there is for love. We are so often weighed down; we need to empty ourselves of what is burdening us so that God can fill us with his peace, love, joy and happiness. To empty ourselves, we need to be able to forgive. The more we can forgive, the more we empty ourselves and the more love we are capable of receiving.

I want to suggest four areas where we can practice forgiveness in our lives. The first is with people close to us.

Who are the people close to you in life? Family members, friends, neighbours, colleagues, and people you encounter casually each day. It is inevitable that from time to time we will have disputes with some of these people. Family fallouts can begin with a row over who is doing the washing up and escalate into something much more serious. Similarly with our friends there can be differences of opinions that start out as petty but, if not addressed, can result in underlying resentments. Neighbours can have disagreements over issues like parking, land, rights of way, children and so on.

If you are hurting as a result of a dispute with someone in your close circle of daily life, as a follower of Jesus Christ and from the example of Matt Talbot's life you are called upon to forgive, to empty that hurt, so that you can experience and be filled with the love of God. Forgivness is never easy, especially if the injury caused was a very serious one. Therefore, in trying to forgive, it is important to recognise that forgiveness is an act which will not always be accompanied by comfortable feelings of warmth and positivity. You may still feel angry with the person but you decide not to act on that anger nor allow it to continue to colour your judgement. To forgive does not imply that the offence which is being forgiven was acceptable. Rather it is to begin again in the relationship, wiser and more bruised, but determined to move forward in hope.

Anger with God is a second area which may feature in our lives. If someone close to us dies, or we experience the pain of broken relationships, it is tempting to blame God. When we can't find a solution to our problems and difficulties, we can turn on God, and like the prophet Jeremiah in the Old Testament we curse the day of our birth.

It is an unfortunate trait of human nature to take our anger out on those closest to us. Like our loved ones, God does not escape our wrath. The difference with God is that he doesn't fight back; he takes it from us with a smile. He loves us. He understands our needs. But if we reflect on how much God loves and forgives us when we fail, we need to ask ourselves if we really believe that God is responsible for the hurt or the mess in our lives. If we think about it, we can see that sometimes our own actions have contributed to our problems. And very often, no one is to blame at all. God suffers with us in our pain but God never causes our distress so perhaps we need to let go of our misplaced anger, release the energy it takes to stay angry and channel it into allowing love and mercy to rule our thoughts and actions.

The need to forgive authority is a third area to consider. For the good order of society, authority is necessary. From the very moment of birth, we are all subject to authority from parents. At school, that authority is extended to teachers and those in charge. In the community, various government agencies take different responsibilities for authority. As we grow older, we ourselves also assume positions of authority, which demand responsibility and accountability from us.

Authority demands a certain level of trust and respect. If you have been treated well by someone, their respect will remain with you; it is something you will not forget. Likewise if you have been hurt by someone, it will not be forgotten either.

Many people carry a hurt from the past perpetuated by an authority figure. It may have been a parent, teacher, priest or other official but because trust was broken, it can lead to immense pain. If you are hurting in such a way, it is important to talk through the hurt with a trusted friend or counsellor so that it can no longer diminish your life or have power over how you view others or yourself.

The final area of forgiveness is perhaps the most difficult and it is forgiveness of self.

So often we do things that we regret. We hurt the people we love the most. When this happens we should seek forgiveness and try to makes amends for the pain we have caused. Then we should resolve to move forward and not allow our weaknesses to paralyse us by dwelling on the negative parts of ourselves We can take comfort from the figure of Jesus on the cross as he cried out 'Father, forgive them for they know not what they do'. If Jesus could offer such all-encompassing mercy, we should not deny it to ourselves by becoming blind to the value we hold within us as children of God.

The gospel we are trying to follow every day is a Gospel of Love. Despite our weaknesses and failings, once we can empty ourselves of what is weighing us down, the love and mercy of God can do great things for us. Matt Talbot has shown us that when he emptied himself and embraced the God of Love, his whole life blossomed and transformed.

PRAYER

God of mercy and compassion, teach us that even if our hearts condemn us, you do not. Father of mercy and God of all consolation, you do not wish the sinner to die but to be converted and live. Bless, enlighten and sustain with your Holy Spirit all of us in our journey of forgiveness. When we forgive, we free ourselves of the burden of bitterness and we free the other person of the burden of guilt. We know, Lord, that our forgiveness must come from the heart, which means it must be true, sincere and genuine. A cold forgiveness is not much use.

BE RECONCILED

Help us to start forgiving now;
putting it off only deepens the
wound, prolongs bitterness and
postpones happiness. Life is short;
time is fleeting and today is the day
to forgive.
Lord, deliver us from the poison of
bitterness and give us the grace to
forgive from the heart those who
have offended us. Then we will know
and realise the warmth of your
forgiveness.

Venerable Matt Talbot, pray for us.

7

The Eucharist:
Nourishment for Life

Jesus, with the power of the
Spirit in him, returned to
Galilee and his reputation
spread throughout the
countryside. He taught in their
synagogues and everyone
praised him. He came to
Nazareth, where he had been
brought up, and went into the
synagogue on the Sabbath day
as he usually did. He stood up to
read, and they handed him the
scroll of the prophet Isaiah.
Unrolling the scroll he found
the place where it is written:
'The spirit of the Lord has been
given to me, for he has anointed
me. He has sent me to bring the
good news to the poor, to

proclaim liberty to captives and to the blind new sight, to set the downtrodden free, to proclaim the Lord's year of favour.' He then rolled up the scroll, gave it back to the assistant and sat down. And all eyes in the synagogue were fixed on him. Then he began to speak to them, 'This text is being fulfilled today even as you listen'.

Luke 4:14-21

It is a sad but well-documented fact that the number of people attending daily or weekly Mass continues to decline. Many people report that while they believe in God, they no longer go to church. Whatever the reasons for their decision, St Paul would see their absence as a loss to the whole faith community. For Paul, all of us make up the Body of Christ. We belong together, we need each other, and we need to come together in prayer.

For many years, Matt Talbot lived only for himself. His addiction to alcohol copper-fastened his attitude that he could make it alone. It was only in the second half of his life, when he found sobriety, that he also found an appreciation for the Eucharist, the need to come together, the need to be with others, with Christ at the centre. Each day of his life began with Mass and he found great support from the Eucharist and allowed it to impact strongly on his life and thinking.

In our gospel passage we are told that Jesus went to the synagogue on the Sabbath Day as he usually did. Those words 'as he usually did' tell us a lot about Jesus and the importance he placed on praying together, belonging together. If Jesus felt the need to gather with others in prayer, it tells us how crucial it is for us to gather as a community that cares for one another and that has a vision for a shared future.

On Jesus' visit to the synagogue he reads from the prophet Isaiah and presents what could be called a Christian manifesto for living. It has much to offer us as we consider its application today.

The Spirit of the Lord has been given to me

Just think of this for a moment; try to take it in: the spirit of the Lord is in each one of us and with God's spirit in us, everything is possible. This is a reassurance that we can take courage from as we struggle with the failings and difficulties of our lives.

Good News to the Poor

Gospel means 'good news' and the entire gospel story is the good news of God's unending love for his people. As believers in this good news, we are asked to stand in unity with those whose lives are impoverished whether through addiction, exploitation or through being denied the very basics of life.

Liberty to Captives

Jesus was not talking about opening or emptying our prisons, but about helping all people to be free to live to the full, no longer bound by the chains of destructive behaviours.

New Sight

Jesus invites us to see the beauty and the fragility in all life; to see that the scars of our inadequacies or compulsions can make up rich and beautiful images if we learn from our failures and use the threads of our mistakes to create new, more complete tapestries.

Set the Downtrodden Free

There are few more downtrodden than those enslaved by addictions which stifle their lives, belittle their potential and destroy their relationships. The first step in conquering such affliction is to accept that the problem exists and has taken control. Only then can further steps along the slow road to recovery be made. Only then can denial be left behind, the impulse to 'go it alone' be rejected and the company of fellow travellers in one's family, faith community, addiction support group, be embraced.

Declare the Lord's Year of Favour

Life is to be celebrated and enjoyed. We pray in the Eucharist that the Lord be with you, believing that the Lord is very much within each one of us. With so many trapped by a harmful habit, whether be it over-work, over-eating, over-exercising or excessive alcohol consumption, they are deprived of experiencing the joys of life, unable to enjoy the Lord's favours and blessings.

Every time we gather to celebrate Mass together, as Matt Talbot discovered, it offers us strength from Jesus truly present in the Eucharist, in the sacred scripture and in the assembly gathered as his Body. Through praying together as a community we are able to re-commit to the manifesto entrusted to us by Christ. It enables us to find the courage to 'go forth to love and serve the Lord' through confronting our own demons, to move beyond them and to reach out in solidarity to the poor, the vulnerable and the downtrodden, knowing that the Spirit of the Lord is with us to be our guide.

PRAYER

Lord, Jesus Christ, you gave us the Eucharist as your gift to us. May our participation in the Eucharist help us to experience the Sprit of God alive in our lives. May our gathering with others to share the word of God and to share in the one bread and the one cup help us to experience the salvation you won for us and the peace of the kingdom where you live with the Father and the Holy Spirit for ever. Amen

Venerable Matt Talbot, pray for us.

8

Mary:
Comfort of the Afflicted

There was a wedding at Cana in Galilee. The mother of Jesus was there, and Jesus and his disciples had also been invited. When they ran out of wine, the mother of Jesus said to him, 'They have no wine'. Jesus said, 'Woman why turn to me? My hour has not come yet'. His mother said to the servants, 'Do whatever he tells you'.

There were six stone water jars standing there, meant for the ablutions that are customary among the Jews: each could hold twenty or thirty gallons. Jesus said to the servants, 'Fill the jars with water', and they filled them to the brim. 'Draw some out now,' he told them, 'and take them to the steward.' They did this: the steward tasted the water, and it had turned into wine.

Having no idea where it came from – only the servants who had drawn the water knew – the steward called the bridegroom and said, 'People generally serve the best wine first, and keep the cheaper sort till the guests have had plenty to drink, but you have kept the best wine till now.'

This was the first of the signs given by Jesus: it was given at Cana in Galilee. He let this glory be seen, and his disciples believed in him.

John 2:1-11

Matt Talbot lived on this earth for sixty-nine years and one month, and during his lifetime Our Lady made three appearances on the earth. When Matt was just two years old, in 1858 Mary appeared to St Bernadette at Lourdes with her message of prayer and penance. When Matt was twenty-three years old, in 1879 Mary appeared in Knock, County Mayo, and at the age of sixty-one she appeared to the children of Fatima in Portugal.

The daily prayer for most Catholics in Ireland at that time was the Rosary. The Religious orders that came to Ireland from Europe brought their Marian devotion with them. So it comes as no surprise that Matt Talbot had a great devotion to Mary. The messages emanating from Lourdes, Knock and Fatima were a call to repentance, prayer and penance, which Matt wholeheartedly embraced in his life.

Very little is written about Mary in the four gospels or in the Acts of the Apostles, but short as her story is, she comes across as a woman of independence, strength, care and of love and concern. These are qualities that Matt tried to imitate in his own life.

In our gospel passage of the Wedding Feast of Cana, Mary is often described as 'Our Lady of the Elbow', for giving a nudge to her son Jesus to do something to help a couple in need. That elbow continues to be given to all of us by the care and love we receive from others in our journey through life.

The late Pope John Paul II wrote an encyclical letter entitled *Redemptoris Mater*, Mother of the Redeemer. This encyclical letter broadens our understanding of Mary's place in the life of the Church. The document points out that Mary was the first to believe, from the moment of the Annunciation and Conception, through to the birth of Christ at Bethlehem. And she continued to believe all through the hidden years in Nazareth and, above all, during the tragic experience of Calvary. Not even beneath the cross did Mary's faith fail.

Whilst prayer was important for Matt Talbot, the best way he could express his devotion to Mary was to live by the example she set in her life: her story provides lessons we too can learn.

Her Example as Mother

The image of Mary standing at the foot of the cross as her son's life ebbed away is one of heart-rending poignancy. Though his friends abandoned him, she remained, steadfast in her love and total in her faith. She is a guide for all mothers when the actions of their children confuse or dismay. She shows that in the face of suffering, all we are asked to do is love. We may not always agree or condone but, following Mary's example, we must always love. Michelangelo's famous *Pietà* shows Mary with the dead body of her son Jesus across her knees after he was taken down from the cross. It depicts in visual form the love of a mother for her son.

There are many *Pietà* scenes in our world today, where parents, families and friends receive the bodies of loved ones who have died because of addictions, with all the sadness and heartbreak which that entails. Mary has gone before us along the road of suffering. She is a guide and support through any pilgrimage of pain and grief. She is truly the comforter of the afflicted and we can turn to her always with confidence.

Her Example of Concern

Mary was a woman for others and even from the little that the gospels tell us of her we can see the concern she showed throughout her life: for her cousin Elizabeth whom she immediately went to visit even though she herself was pregnant, for the newly married couple at Cana and for the disciples, whom she remained with in spite of their disloyalty and fear. May her concern be a model for us as we witness to Mary in the action of our lives.

Her Example of Strength

Mary must have been a strong person. One of the most difficult situations in life is to watch our loved ones suffer. How often is this the experience of family, friends, neighbours and colleagues as they helplessly watch a loved one destroy their life, knowing that they are powerless until the addict first recognises their compulsion. Until then, great strength is required in trying to support a fellow human being with an addiction.

At the wedding feast of Cana we hear the last recorded words of Mary in scripture: 'Do whatever he tells you.' They are words that we can take to heart in the midst of the turmoil of life.

Her Great Example of Hope

In our struggles with addictions and in sharing the life with people who have addictions the one thing we all cling to is hope: hope for a better future. Mary, God's mother and our mother, is the great figure of hope. Matt Talbot realised this very early in his struggle to be set free, clinging to Mary as a woman of hope. Mary has been assumed body and soul into heaven. One creature, and one creature alone, has broken the death barrier between earth and heaven. Where she has gone, we hope one day to follow.

Devotion to Mary has been a feature of our Church since its foundation on Pentecost Sunday. The Council of Ephesus in 431 venerated Mary as the Mother of God. Mary has always received respect and esteem in every generation. She has inspired some of the greatest artists in the world, painters and sculptors, to create some of their most wonderful work. In our struggles today with addictions such defining influences are welcome and give us hope.

In Matt Talbot's daily prayer life, the beautiful prayer of the Angelus was prayed twice each day as the bells from the various churches in Dublin rang out at 12 noon and 6 p.m. The Angelus is a beautiful, simple and scriptural prayer based on St Luke's gospel account of the Annunciation. In this, the twenty-first century, the Angelus bell continues to peal on our national television and radio station at 12 noon and 6 p.m., as well as in many churches around the country. It is a call to respond in prayer, wherever we may be.

In praying the Angelus, we pray the Hail Mary. In this prayer we acknowledge Mary as a woman full of grace and close to God, and then we ask for her help in two most important moments of life: the present, and the hour of our death. The story of Matt Talbot's life tells us how important the present moment was for him and the moment of death which came for him on the way to Mass on Trinity Sunday, 7 June 1925.

PRAYER

The Angel of the Lord declared to Mary.

Response:
And she conceived of the Holy Spirit.
Hail Mary, full of grace,
the Lord is with thee,
blessed art thou among women,
and blessed is the fruit of thy womb, Jesus.
Holy Mary, mother of God,
pray for us, sinners,
now and at the hour of our death.
Amen.

Behold the handmaid of the Lord.

Response:
Be it done to me according to your word.
Hail Mary ...

And the word was made flesh.

Response:
And dwelt among us.
Hail Mary ...

Pray for us, O Holy Mother of God.

Response:
That we may be made worthy of the promises of Christ.

Let us pray:
Pour forth, we beseech you O Lord, your grace into our hearts that we, to whom the incarnation of Christ, your son, was made known by the message of an angel, may be brought by his passion and cross to the glory of his resurrection, through the same Christ our Lord. Amen.

9

Count Your Blessings: Celebrating Life

On the way to Jerusalem, Jesus travelled along the border between Samaria and Galilee. As he entered one of the villages, ten lepers came to meet him. They stood some way off and called to him, 'Jesus! Master! Take pity on us'. When he saw them, he said, 'Go and show yourselves to the priests'. Now as they were going away they were cleansed. Finding himself cured, one of them turned back praising God at the top of his voice and threw himself at the feet of Jesus and thanked him. The man was a Samaritan. This made Jesus say, 'Were not all ten made clean?

The other nine, where are they?' It seemed that no one had come back to give praise to God, except this foreigner. And he said to the man, 'Stand up and go on your way. Your faith has saved you'.

Luke 17:11-19

Often, and especially at difficult moments, we say 'count your blessings'. What do we mean by a blessing? In one sense it means the raising up of a person or a thing to the service of God, setting it apart from worldly values. A church may be blessed very solemnly, a rosary beads simply and, of course, through the sacraments of initiation, we are all blessed and welcomed into God's family in ever-deepening ways.

In a general way, a blessing is quite simply a gift from God. We can be blessed with good health, with good fortune, with talents, good friends, with a happy family life.

Blessings are found throughout the scriptures. In the book of Genesis, the first book in the Bible, Melchizedek, the priest, meets Abraham, who after an important victory praises and blesses God (13:18-20).

The Beatitudes remind us of being blessed, thankful and fortunate.

St Paul and the evangelists in the New Testament refer to the blessings which Jesus said over bread at the Last Supper and when he fed the multitude. In each case, it is a prayer of thanksgiving for God's goodness (Corinthians 11:23-26; Luke 9:11-17). Such thanksgiving has a long tradition in Irish spirituality when, in everyday conversation, we would acknowledge God and his goodness simply by saying 'Thanks be to God'.

Everything which occurs in the course of our human lives can be viewed as a blessing, even if all occurrences are not necessarily pleasant. I am sure that even suffering is a blessing, despite the difficulty of accepting troubled people and adverse circumstances in our live. Whilst suffering can hardly be called good in itself, many find that the experience of suffering matures us and makes us more empathic and accepting of others. In this sense suffering can be turned into good and seen as a gift.

The hardest arithmetic to master is the one that asks us to 'count our blessings'. Yet if we are honest with ourselves, however deep our present challenges are, however seemingly terrible our current troubles, however apparently irremovable our long-standing frustrations, most of us have more blessings in this life than we usually acknowledge. Part of our Irish tradition shows us that men, women and children have always thanked God for their creation, and indeed preservation, and for all the blessings of life, promising to respond in gratitude, not only with words, but also by deeds, by the type of life lived.

If we were to keep a diary of daily living and record all that happens each day of our lives, we would be pleasantly surprised with all our blessings and the results at the end of the day might even amaze us. St Paul tells us that we walk by faith, not by sight, and he reminds us to give thanks, whatever happens. In times of addiction and its related suffering, even on the darkest day, being aware of the blessings of our lives can be spiritually and psychologically uplifting and at times even vital. If we can go to sleep at night having thought of five things we could be thankful for during that day, however trivial, we will wake up the next day more positive in outlook and more able to face the new day.

In the gospel parable of the ten lepers being healed, nine took Jesus for granted and got on with the business of their lives. One came back to say thank you to Jesus and Jesus appreciated it. So often, we take God and others for granted. In the story of Matt Talbot's life, he became very aware, through prayer, of how much God loved him and blessed him. In this decision to abstain from alcohol and develop his prayer life, he found great confidence and hope. Every day of his life, he thanked God the Almighty for hearing his prayer, for giving him hope and the opportunity to re-focus his life and to recognise the difference between what is important and what is trivial.

May God continue to shower his blessings on us and on all in need and may we never forget that God created us in his image and continues to love us.

PRAYER

Thank you God for all that you have given us.
Thank you God for all that you have taken away from us.
Thank you God for all that you have left us.

Heavenly father, help us to:
Count our blessings instead of our
crosses;
Count our gains instead of our losses;
Count our joys instead of our woes;
Count our friends instead of our foes;
Count our courage instead of our
fears;
Count our laughs instead of our tears;
Count our kind deeds instead of our
selfishness;
Count our health instead of our
wealth;
Count on God instead of ourselves.

Venerable Matt Talbot, pray for us.

Further Reading

Simon O'Byrne OFM, *Matt Talbot: Secular Franciscan*, Veritas, 1979.

Mary Purcell, *The Making of Matt Talbot*, Messenger Publications, 1972.